THE CHILEAN MINERS
Buried Alive

BY YVONNE PEARSON

Published by The Child's World®
1980 Lookout Drive • Mankato, MN 56003-1705
800-599-READ • www.childsworld.com

Acknowledgments
The Child's World®: Mary Berendes, Publishing Director
Red Line Editorial: Design, editorial direction, and production
Photographs ©: Jorge Saenz/AP Images, cover, 1; Thomas Sykora/Shutterstock
Images, 4; Red Line Editorial, 6; Marcelo Hernandez/DPA/Corbis, 8; STR/Reuters/
Corbis, 10; Jose Manuel De La Maza/Handout/DPA/Corbis, 12; Martin Mejia/AP
Images, 14; Government of Chile/Handout/Corbis, 16; Cezaro de Luca/EPA/Corbis,
19; Reinhold Matay/AP Images, 20

ISBN 9781634074735

LCCN 2015946320

Printed in the United States of America
Mankato, MN
December, 2015
PA02286

ABOUT THE AUTHOR

Yvonne Pearson is an author and a social worker. She has written poetry,
essays, and books. She loves to write because it lets her keep learning
new things.

TABLE OF
CONTENTS

Chapter 1

THE MINE COLLAPSES

The morning of August 5, 2010, was like any other morning for miners going into the San José mine. They got out of bed, got dressed, and ate breakfast. Those who had families probably told them they'd see them in the evening and wished them a good day. But for the miners, this would not be an ordinary day.

The San José mine is located in Chile. Chile is a long, narrow country on the southwest side of South America. The miners worked in the mountain. They **extracted** gold and copper from the earth.

The miners rode almost an hour through the Atacama Desert to the mine. Fields of tiny purple flowers spread over the pale desert hills. When they reached the entrance to the mine, it looked like a big mouth with stone teeth. The men rode to the mine in pickup trucks on a rough road. It twisted downward for almost 4 miles (6.4 km).

The San José mine was known for being a dangerous place to work. The men were used to hearing rocks falling. On this particular day, the noise of falling rocks seemed unusually bad. "The mine is weeping a lot," the miners would say to each other.[1]

The last men entered the mine around 1:00 p.m. that day. Soon after that, the mountain began to cave in. A 700,000-ton (635,029-T) **diorite** rock broke off the mountain. It was falling through the layers of the mine. The rock was roughly the shape of a gigantic ship. It weighed 150 times more than the *Titanic*. In fact, it weighed almost twice as much as the Empire State Building.

One of the miners, Franklin Lobos, said the collapse hit them as a roar of sound. An explosive blast raced down the tunnels. Rocks rained down. The mountain shook. The eruption brought a

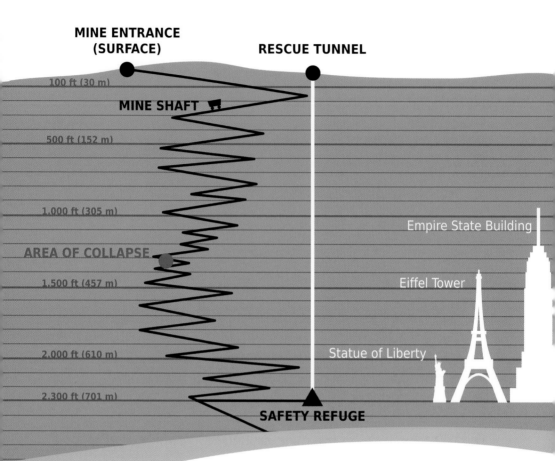

MINE ENTRANCE
(SURFACE)

RESCUE TUNNEL

100 ft (30 m)

MINE SHAFT

500 ft (152 m)

1,000 ft (305 m)

Empire State Building

AREA OF COLLAPSE

1,500 ft (457 m)

Eiffel Tower

2,000 ft (610 m)

Statue of Liberty

2,300 ft (701 m)

SAFETY REFUGE

▲ A diagram of the mine shows
just how far the miners were
trapped underground.

cloud of dust with it, blinding the miners. The blast threw Victor
Zamora against a wall and knocked out several of his teeth. Omar
Reygadas said, "I thought my eyes were going to pop out of my
head."[2] The collapse blocked the road that led out of the mine.
For more than two hours, rocks kept tumbling like dominoes
down through the deep layers inside the mine.

In the midst of the collapse, the men fought their way to a safety refuge at the bottom of the mine. It was a room carved out of the rock. It had a white tile floor, two oxygen tanks, a cabinet with some old medicine, and a little bit of food. When things had settled down, a small escape party left the safety refuge to search for a way out. They found a **ventilation shaft** that was open to the surface. They began to climb the ladder that was put there for emergencies. However, the mining company had not installed the ladder all the way to the top. They had to return to the safety refuge in defeat.

The 33 men were buried together 2,300 feet (701 m)—about a half-mile—under the ground. They were surrounded by darkness. The men had only the dim lights of their headlamps to guide them. There was no way for the miners to let anyone know they were alive. Trapped in the belly of the mine, it was the beginning of a long ordeal. In the belly of the mine, there would be no sunlight for these men for 69 days.

Chapter 2

BURIED ALIVE

The trapped miners were frightened, hungry, sweaty, and coated with dust. But they made plans and organized themselves. There was almost no food in the refuge. What little food they had needed to last as long as possible. They ate only once a day.

Each meal was a spoonful of tuna with a little milk and water, and one or two cookies.

◄ Rescuers stood near the entrance of the mine waiting for news on the miners.

The miners drank all their clean water in the first day. After that, they had to drink industrial water—water in which they had washed their dirty gloves, and even taken baths. The water even had drops of motor oil in it.

The men felt very discouraged. Still, they stayed brave and kept their spirits up. They joked with each other. They did exercises. The miners were of different faiths, but they gathered for prayer every day. They were careful about each other's feelings.

HOW THEY SURVIVED

The following is all the food that was in the safety refuge when the mine collapsed. The 33 men had to share this food for 17 days:

- 93 packages of cookies (chocolate and lemon flavored sandwich creams)
- One can of salmon
- One can of peaches
- One can of peas
- 18 cans of tuna
- 24 liters of milk
- 10 liters of bottled water

By the end of the 17 days, the men were surviving on only one cookie each every other day.

They would apologize when they made mistakes. The men became almost like a family.

One day, the miners had a picnic. They made a fire and heated water. Then they added tuna and their only can of peas to the pot. Mario Sepúlveda was known for his energetic and enthusiastic personality. He declared, "We're going to show that we are Chileans of the heart. And we're going to have a delicious soup today."[3] The men had a cell phone, but it did not work so deep in the mine. Instead, they used the camera on the phone to make a video of their picnic. Sepúlveda left a message on the video for his 13-year-old son. He said, "Francisco, when God tells you to be a warrior, this is what it means to be a warrior."[4]

Three days after the collapse, the men heard the sound of a drill. They knew that a rescue crew was trying to find them. They heard the drill in the distance day after day. The men grew hungrier and weaker.

The miners lost weight. Their cheeks became hollow. Their eyes sank into their skulls. They had long, crazy dreams. One of the men suffered temporary blindness from hunger. Many of the miners assumed that they would die in the mine. A miner named Victor Segovia kept a diary. He wrote: "I am weak, and very hungry. I'm suffocating . . . it feels like I'm going to go

◄ Family members held each other for comfort as they continued to wait for the rescue of the miners.

▲ Chilean President Sebastián Piñera held the note from the miners that proved they were alive.

crazy." After the rescue, Reygadas said, "I'm not embarrassed to say I cried a lot . . . thinking I wouldn't see my family again, and thinking of the suffering they would go through."[5] Some of the miners wrote farewell letters to their families.

Then one day, the drilling became extremely loud. The miners' hopes rose. The men prepared a note that said, *Estamos bien en el refugio. Los 33.* ("We are well in the refuge. The 33.") The miners were excited when they saw the drill break through the ceiling. To signal those a half-mile (0.8 km) above them that they were alive, they hit the drill like children pounding a **piñata**. They attached their note to the drill. Then they celebrated. They sang the national anthem. They chanted "Chi-chi-chi, le-le-le, mineros de Chile!"[6]

The day the mine collapsed, the men's families had gathered at the mine. They waited to see if the miners were found. The families made a tent city. They slept and ate there, keeping watch for their miners. The city became known as Camp Hope. It was also filled with journalists who were telling the whole world about the rescue efforts. Everyone celebrated when the drill pulled the note back up. They waved flags, hugged, cried, and laughed. There were bonfires, music, and dancing.

It was 17 days since the men had been buried. Everyone was deliriously happy to find out that they were alive. But the miners were still stranded in their deep black hole in the earth. It was a long, dangerous waiting game to see if the miners could ever be saved.

Chapter 3

WAITING

The rescue team drilled **boreholes** 3.5 inches (8.9 cm) in **diameter** through almost a half-mile (0.8 km) of rock to find the miners. It would take six more weeks to make one of the boreholes big enough to fit a man. The hole needed to be almost 2 feet (0.6 m) in diameter. Then the crew would lower a bullet-shaped capsule that could rescue the miners one by one.

These skinny boreholes became lifelines for the miners.
A slender, 6-foot-long (1.8-m) plastic tube called *la paloma*
(the pigeon) was lowered through the holes. It was stuffed with
water, food, medicine, toothpaste, shampoo, soap, and other
important things. The tube also carried letters from the miners to
their families.

The rescue crew lowered wires to hook up a telephone and
a video system. The families talked to the men and sent love
and encouragement. Doctors gave advice. Chilean President
Sebastián Piñera offered reassurance. The men learned that the
whole world was watching and waiting for their rescue.

It was a long, hard wait in that small room. Because it was
so deep in the earth, it was as hot and humid as a jungle. Now,
trapped inside, sweat ran off them continuously. With the food
lowered to them through the boreholes, the 33 miners had the
energy to work hard again. They patrolled for falling rocks and
reinforced ceilings and walls. They also drained away water
and repaired communication equipment. The men entertained
themselves by playing cards and dominoes as they waited
desperately for the drilling to reach them.

Chapter 4

THE RESCUE

On the 65th day of the miners' ordeal, they saw a drill break through again. This time, it opened an escape tunnel for them. It was 8:00 a.m. on October 9. To the men, it was a wonderful sight.

But the rescue tunnel caused a new problem. It brought fresh, cool air to the men, which made the rock in the mountain contract. The mine began to crack and groan again. This was worrisome. Before the rescue could begin, the shaft had to be inspected. Casing had to be installed in some parts for safety. This took four more days.

On the 69th day after the mine collapsed, the men were finally lifted to safety. It was almost midnight. The rescue capsule was lowered inside the mine. Florencio Avalos was the first to climb into the tube. He was physically fit, so the rescuers thought he

SAN JOSÉ MINE

The San José mine had a history of accidents. Small altars in the main tunnel marked spots where workers had been killed. In fact, in the 12 years before the big collapse, eight men had been killed at the mine. The mine was forced to shut down after a geologist was killed in 2007. The mining company was ordered to make safety improvements, but the government let the company start operating again without having completed the safety measures. Then, just two months before the collapse, there was another accident. A miner lost his leg when a rock fell on him.

could handle any problems more easily than the other miners. The capsule was so narrow that it just fit around Avalos' body. The door closed on him. Then a winch, a machine used to lift an object, pulled him up. For 15 minutes he swooshed and turned as the capsule lurched upward like a carnival ride. Avalos' family awaited him anxiously at the top. His nine-year-old son, Byron, broke down in tears when he saw his father pulled from the capsule. A hug told him that his father was safe.

Next came the **exuberant** Sepúlveda. When he got to the top, he led the crowd in a cheer. He said in an interview that evening, "I was with God and the devil, and they fought over me. God won."[7]

Hour after hour, the capsule delivered the men to the fresh night air, then into fresh daytime air. Almost 24 hours after Avalos arrived, the last man, Luis Urzúa, stepped out of the capsule. Urzúa was the shift foreman in charge of the workers when the mine collapsed. When he got to the top he shook hands with President Piñera and said, "Mr. President, my shift is over."[8]

The rescue capsule that brought the miners to safety was ▶ 13 feet (3.9 m) tall and just 21 inches (53 cm) wide.

Chapter 5

THE AFTERMATH

In the first year after the rescue, the miners were treated like celebrities. They were flown all over the world to give speeches and interviews, and to be honored. Some were even given money by a local businessman to help them as they got their lives back together.

Even though they were considered heroes, the miners soon ran into difficulties. Many of them have suffered from terrible nightmares, anxiety, and flashbacks about their ordeal. The miners have also had trouble getting jobs. Many mine owners have not wanted to hire them. They were afraid that the men would be mentally scarred or would complain about safety violations. Many of the 33 are now poorer than they were before the collapse.

A Chilean Congressional Commission conducted an investigation in 2011. They found the mine owners responsible for the collapse. The commission said the mine owners did not put enough safety measures in place. The investigation also found that the Chilean mine safety agency did not properly enforce safety regulations.

Chilean **prosecutors** considered bringing criminal charges against the mining company. However, in August 2013, they announced that they were dropping all charges. The prosecutors said they found no legal reasons to justify any action against the company. Many of the miners are now pursuing a lawsuit against the company and the government. Despite the many problems and disappointments, the 33 miners are still considered heroes. The men are alive today because of their incredible **fortitude**.

GLOSSARY

boreholes (BOOR-hols): Boreholes are deep, narrow holes drilled into the ground to locate things, to take out samples, or to release gas or water and other liquids. Companies might drill boreholes to find oil.

diameter (die-AM-eh-tur): A diameter is the straight line that goes across the middle of a circle. The diameter of the hole that led the miners out of the mine was 2 feet (0.6 m).

diorite (DIE-o-rite): Diorite is a type of rock that is dark and coarse-grained. The boulder that fell in the mountain was diorite rock.

extracted (ex-STRAK-ted): Extracted is when something is removed or taken out of its normal place. The miners' job was to extract copper from the mountain.

exuberant (ex-OOB-ur-ant): Exuberant is when someone is overflowing with joy and liveliness. Despite being trapped, some miners stayed exuberant throughout the ordeal.

fortitude (FORT-ih-tood): Fortitude is having the mental and emotional strength to face difficulty with courage. The men were recognized for the fortitude they had while being trapped underground.

piñata (peen-YAH-tah): A piñata is a figure made of papier-mâché that is filled with candy or toys and suspended in the air so that children may use sticks to break it open. The miners hit the drill with excitement as if it were a piñata.

prosecutors (PRAH-suh-cue-tores): Prosecutors try to prove in court that a person accused of a crime is guilty. Chilean prosecutors fought hard to try and get justice for the miners.

ventilation shaft (vent-i-LA-shun SHAFT): A ventilation shaft is an open passageway that lets air in and out. Mines have ventilation shafts to keep the miners safe.

SOURCE NOTES

1. Nick Romeo. "Deep Down Dark Tells the Remarkable Story of 33 Chilean Miners Trapped for 69 days." *The Christian Science Monitor*. The Christian Science Monitor, 15 Oct. 2014. Web. 5 Jun. 2015.

2. Jonathan Franklin. 33 *Men: Inside the Miraculous Survival and Dramatic Rescue of the Chilean Miners*. New York: Berkley Books, 2011. Print. 21.

3. Hector Tobar. "Sixty-Nine Days: The Ordeal of the Chilean Miners." *The New Yorker*. Condé Nast, 7 Jul. 2014. Web. 5 Jun. 2015.

4. Ibid.

5. Ibid.

6. Ibid.

7. Jonathan Franklin. *33 Men: Inside the Miraculous Survival and Dramatic Rescue of the Chilean Miners*. New York: Berkley Books, 2011. Print. 21.

8. Ibid. 277.

TO LEARN MORE

Books

Aronson, Marc. *Trapped: How the World Rescued 33 Miners from 2,000 Feet Below the Chilean Desert*. New York: Atheneum Books for Young Readers, 2011.

Burgan, Michael. *Chile*. Secaucus, NJ: Scholastic Library Publishing, 2009.

Gordon, Nick. *Coal Miner*. Minneapolis, MN: Bellwether Media, 2013.

Scott, Elaine. *Buried Alive!: How 33 Miners Survived 69 Days Deep Under the Chilean Desert*. New York: Clarion Books, 2012.

Web Sites

Visit our Web site for links about the 33 Chilean miners: childsworld.com/links

Note to Parents, Teachers, and Librarians: We routinely verify our Web links to make sure they are safe and active sites. So encourage your readers to check them out!

INDEX